DISNEY LEARNING

WONDERFUL WORLD OF
SHARKS

SCHOLASTIC INC.

As a 2008 Milken Educator, I take the challenge of reviewing educational materials seriously. As I examined the Disney Learning series, I was impressed by the vivid graphics, captivating content, and introductory humor provided by the various Disney characters. But I decided I should take the material to the true experts, my third grade students, and listen to what they had to say. In their words, "The series is interesting. The books are really fun and eye-catching! They make me want to learn more. I can't wait until the books are in the bookstore!" They looked forward to receiving a new book from the series with as much anticipation as a birthday present or a holiday gift. Based on their expert opinion, this series will be a part of my classroom library. I may even purchase two sets to meet their demand.

Barbara Black
2008 Milken Educator
National Board Certified Teacher—Middle Childhood Generalist
Certified 2001/Renewed 2010

ISBN 978-0-545-57273-6

12 11 10 9 8 7 6 5 4 3 2   13 14 15 16 17 18/0

Printed in the U.S.A.   40

First Scholastic printing, April 2013

Written by Christina Wilsdon
Edited by Susan Bishansky
Fact-checked by Barbara Berliner

CONTENTS

WELCOME TO THE

WONDERFUL WORLD OF

SHARKS

AMAZING SHARKS!
From sensitive snout to swishing tail,
a shark is a remarkable creature.

FRIGHTENING CREATURES

Sharks! Most people think sharks are scary. They picture a big, missile-shaped fish with a fin sticking up from its back like a knife. And lots of very sharp teeth!

That image fits *some* sharks—but not all. Sharks can look like fat submarines or flat carpets! Not all sharks are big, either. Some are so small, they can fit in your hand! And believe it or not, most sharks are afraid of people and try to avoid them.

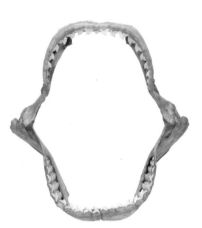

MYSTERIOUS SHARKS

Sharks have roamed the oceans for about 400 million years! Even though they have been around for a long time, we don't know very much about many kinds, or species, of sharks.

Even the most famous shark, the great white, is still a mystery to us. How many are there in the oceans of the world? How often do they have pups? How fast do they grow? How long do they live?

OVERFISHING

Now it's more important than ever to learn about sharks. Many species are at risk of extinction from overfishing. People are catching so many sharks that the fish can't reproduce fast enough to replace the ones taken from the sea. The number of sharks in the oceans is dropping fast.

Sharks are especially hurt by overfishing because they take years to grow up and have pups, and sharks don't have millions of babies like other fish do. Some shark species could be lost forever.

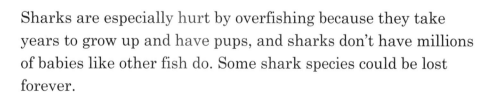

Even though we're still learning about sharks, what we do know about them is amazing! So let's explore the remarkable world of sharks.

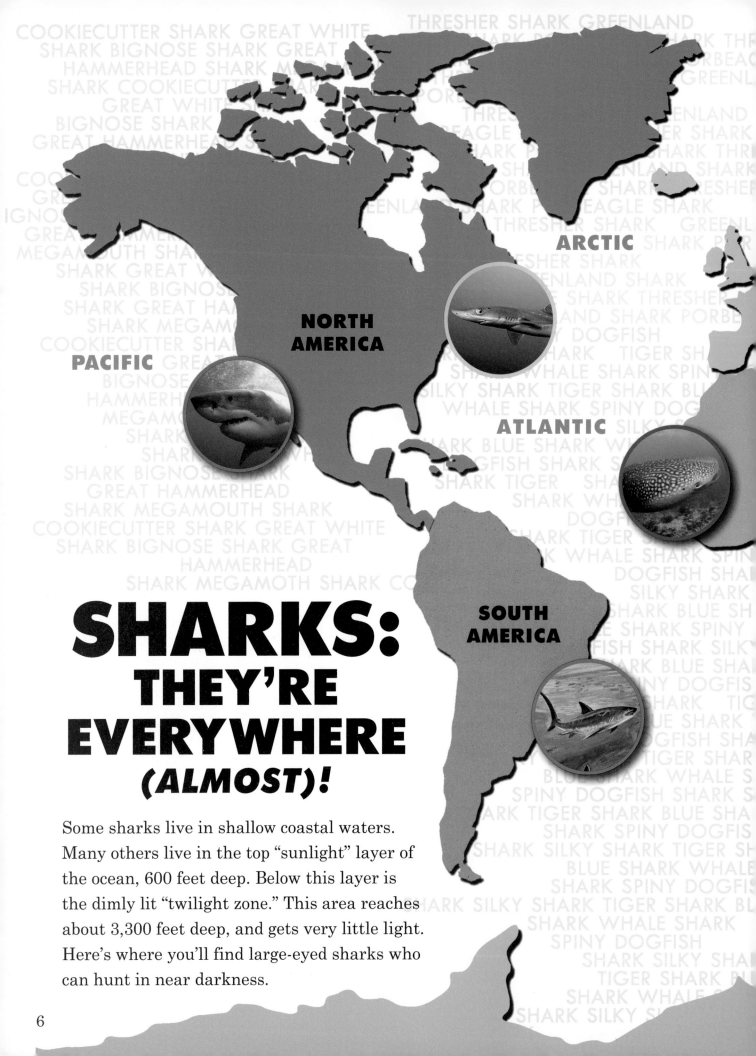

PACIFIC

ARCTIC

NORTH AMERICA

ATLANTIC

SOUTH AMERICA

SHARKS: THEY'RE EVERYWHERE (ALMOST)!

Some sharks live in shallow coastal waters. Many others live in the top "sunlight" layer of the ocean, 600 feet deep. Below this layer is the dimly lit "twilight zone." This area reaches about 3,300 feet deep, and gets very little light. Here's where you'll find large-eyed sharks who can hunt in near darkness.

WHAT IS A SHARK?

A shark is more than just a big fish with lots of sharp teeth.

You can say that again!

Sharks are different from other fish.

HOW ARE SHARKS DIFFERENT FROM OTHER FISH?

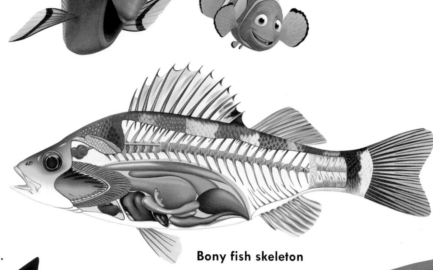

The biggest difference is found **inside** their bodies. Most fish have hard skeletons made of **bone** (scientists call them "bony fish"). A shark's skeleton is made of **cartilage**—the same flexible, rubbery material that's in your own nose and ears. It makes a shark superflexible, too.

Bony fish skeleton

Shark skeleton

WHAT ELSE DO BONY FISH HAVE THAT SHARKS DON'T?

Most bony fish have a "**balloon**" in their bodies that holds air. It's called a **swim bladder**. A fish can add air to its swim bladder when it wants to rise in the water, or it can release air to sink. Sharks don't have a swim bladder. Many have large, **oily livers** instead. Oil is lighter than water, so a shark's liver helps it float.

HOW DO SHARKS AND BONY FISH DIFFER ON THE OUTSIDE?

Fish skin is covered with **scales**, but shark skin isn't. A fish's **gills**—the body part it uses for breathing—are covered by a **bony plate**. A shark's gills aren't. They are attached to slits easily seen on the sides of its head. Also, fish can swim both backward and forward by twisting and turning their **fanlike fins**. A shark can't fold and twirl its fins, so it can only swim forward.

Gills of a lemon shark ▶

9

A SHARK'S BODY

Sharks come in many shapes and sizes, but they all share a basic body plan.

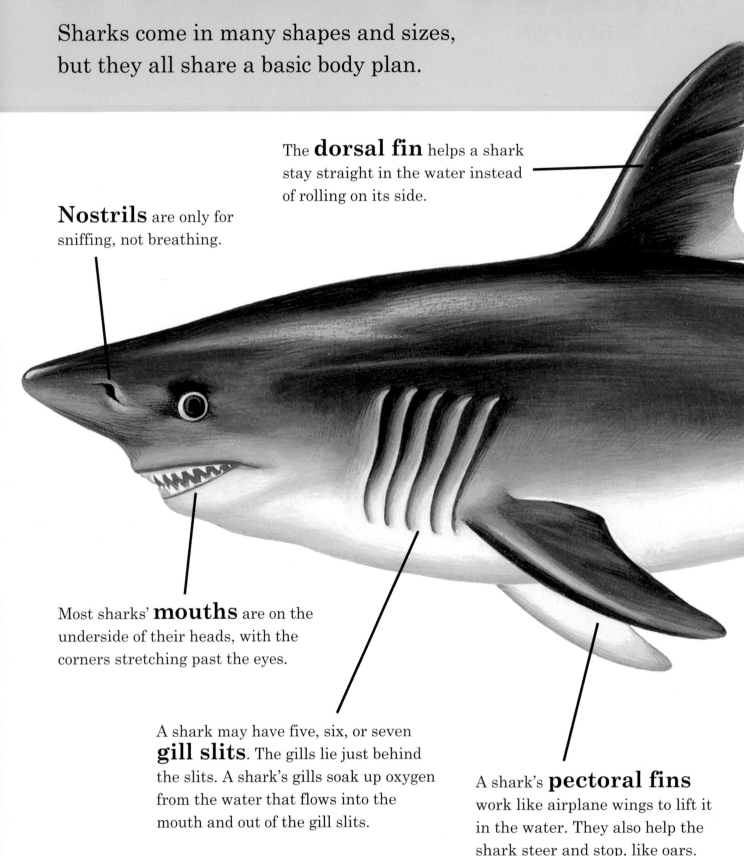

The **dorsal fin** helps a shark stay straight in the water instead of rolling on its side.

Nostrils are only for sniffing, not breathing.

Most sharks' **mouths** are on the underside of their heads, with the corners stretching past the eyes.

A shark may have five, six, or seven **gill slits**. The gills lie just behind the slits. A shark's gills soak up oxygen from the water that flows into the mouth and out of the gill slits.

A shark's **pectoral fins** work like airplane wings to lift it in the water. They also help the shark steer and stop, like oars.

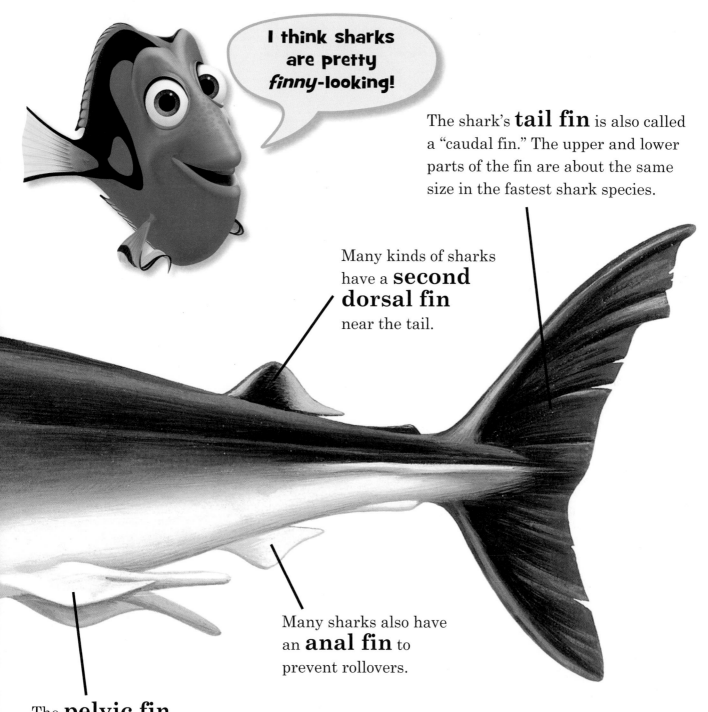

I think sharks are pretty *finny*-looking!

The shark's **tail fin** is also called a "caudal fin." The upper and lower parts of the fin are about the same size in the fastest shark species.

Many kinds of sharks have a **second dorsal fin** near the tail.

Many sharks also have an **anal fin** to prevent rollovers.

The **pelvic fin**, like the dorsal fin, keeps the shark from rolling over.

Sharp shark skin

A shark's skin is covered in "dermal denticles." These toothlike points make shark skin rough, like sandpaper. Denticles are made of the same strong materials as teeth. They help channel water along the shark's body so that it can swim smoothly.

SHARK SHAPES

Round, fat, pointy, flat—sharks come in a wide variety of shapes!

My shape's the best! Just my opinion.

The mako shark's body is shaped like a missile.

Blue shark

Port Jackson shark

HOW ARE SLOWER SHARKS SHAPED?

Sharks that **prowl** the seafloor for crabs, sea urchins, and other slow-moving prey don't need to swim fast. They can be **boxy**, like the **Port Jackson** shark. It has a wide head and powerful, shell-crunching jaws. Or the face can be **round**, like the zebra shark, which looks like a supersized tadpole. They can even be **flat**, like an angel shark, which looks like it's been run over by a **steamroller**. An angel shark can lie flat on the seafloor. It hides there in plain sight, waiting for fish to swim by.

Blue shark

WHICH SHARKS ARE SHAPED LIKE MISSILES?

Sharks that swim fast are shaped like **missiles**—narrow in the front and back, wide and tall in the middle. This pointy shape allows a shark to slip easily through water, like a **knife**. Some sharks with this shape are the great white, **blue**, and mako. Other speedy sea creatures, such as dolphins, have a similar compact shape. (So do speedboats!)

WHAT SHARKS ARE SNAKE-LIKE?

The **frilled shark** looks like an eel with a snake's head. This **slithery** shark lives deep in the ocean, where it ripples through the water hunting for octopus and squid. Its shape helps it **poke** into crevices and between rocks to catch prey.

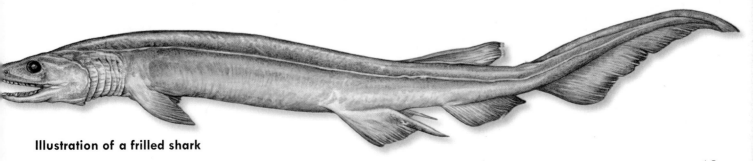

Illustration of a frilled shark

SHARK TEETH

Chomp! Many sharks have lots of razor-sharp teeth—with plenty to spare!

A shark's teeth are replaceable!

What do you call a toothless shark? All shark and no bite!

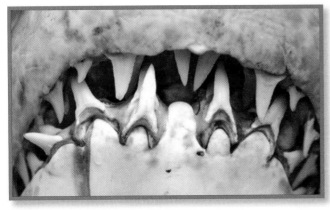
Teeth of a great white shark

WHAT SHAPE
IS A SHARK'S TOOTH?

Each species of shark has **teeth** shaped to catch and eat certain prey. A great white shark's teeth are **triangular**, with rough edges for grabbing and tearing apart large prey such as sea lions. A sand-tiger shark has **needlelike** teeth for seizing slippery fish. A nurse shark has flat, wide teeth for crushing crabs and other shellfish.

Great white shark tooth

HOW MANY
TEETH DOES A SHARK HAVE?

Different kinds of sharks have different numbers of **teeth**. A great white shark, for example, has about **300** teeth. Other species, such as the whale shark, may have a few **thousand**! This is due to the unique setup of a shark's mouth. The teeth sit one behind the other in rows on its **jaws**. A shark may have just a few rows of teeth or as many as 15. Usually just the first row are "**working**" teeth. The other teeth are ready to replace any that fall out.

WHAT HAPPENS IF A SHARK
BREAKS A TOOTH?

A tooth can **break** or **fall out** when a shark bites down hard on its prey. But broken teeth aren't a problem for sharks. A shark's tooth bed is like a **conveyor belt** filled with teeth. If a tooth falls out, a new one moves into its place. Teeth are also regularly **replaced** as they wear down and become dull. A shark may grow and lose more than **20,000 teeth** in its lifetime!

Lower jaw of a great white shark

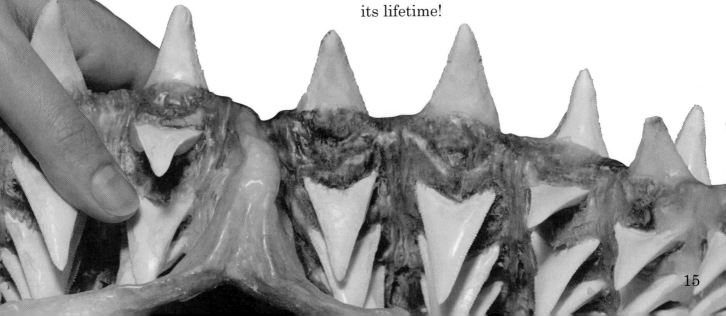

SHARK HEADS

Inside and out, a shark's head
is adapted for catching prey.

**Hammerhead sharks
have unusually
shaped heads.**

A smart shark
always uses
its head!

Great white shark

IS A GREAT WHITE SHARK'S HEAD MOSTLY MOUTH?

The great white does seem to be a bigmouth! That's because a shark's jaws aren't rigidly attached to its **skull**. Jaws are linked to the head by stretchy muscles and cords called **ligaments**. When a great white attacks, it drops its **jaws** and shoves them forward. The shark moves its **snout** up and out of the way. That's why its head seems to disappear when the great white opens its mouth! **Makos** and other sharks that chase prey in wide-open ocean waters have jaws like this, too.

WHAT SHARKS HAVE WEIRDLY SHAPED HEADS?

Many sharks are named for their head shapes. Take the **hammerhead**, for example. Its head is shaped like, well, a hammer! Its eyes sit at either end of its long, flat head. This setup gives the hammerhead superior vision for hunting. The shape also makes the head work like a **wing**, helping the shark turn sharply as it zooms after prey. One hammerhead species, the **winghead**, has a head so wide that it can measure half as long as its body!

WHAT SHARKS HAVE WHALE-LIKE HEADS?

The **whale shark** and **megamouth shark** both have wide, rounded heads like whales. Their mouths are also located up front rather than underneath the head as in most sharks. A whale shark or megamouth's head looks **flat** and **wide** when its mouth is shut. But when it drops its jaw to eat, its head suddenly turns into a tunnel!

Whale shark

Hammerhead shark

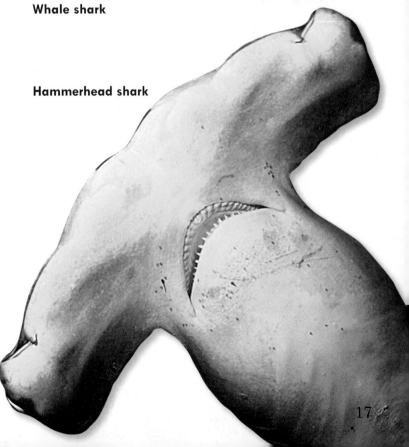

SHARK SENSES

A shark's senses are always
on alert for food or danger.

My senses are
sure on alert
around sharks!

Sharks can see, hear,
taste, smell, and feel!

HOW WELL CAN SHARKS SEE?

Sharks have excellent **eyesight**. Many species can even see in **color**! They also have a **mirrorlike** layer on the backs of their eyes. Light coming into the eye reflects off this layer and shines inside. This "**eyeshine**" makes the eyes extra sensitive, so sharks can see well in dim light. It also makes their eyes glow in the dark when light shines on them! Sharks that live in deep water, such as **bigeye threshers**, have extra-large eyes to help them see better in dark waters.

Whitetip reef shark

Caribbean reef shark

HOW DO SHARKS HEAR AND FEEL?

A shark's **ears** are two small holes on either side of its head. **Vibrations** in the water travel through them to the shark's inner ears. Like all fish, a shark also senses vibrations with its "**lateral lines**." These are like a subway system in the shark's skin. They loop around a shark's head and down its sides. The lines contain hairlike cells that are really sensitive to **motion**. They can detect a wriggling fish from hundreds of feet away!

Tawny nurse shark

CAN SHARKS SMELL AND TASTE?

Yes! A shark smells with its **nostrils**, which are linked directly to parts of its brain. Water flowing in and out of the nostrils is quickly analyzed for **smells**. A shark's sense of smell is so sensitive, it can sniff out one drop of **blood** hidden among a million drops of water! But how can a shark taste food without a fleshy tongue? Easy: it has **taste buds** scattered all over its mouth and throat. Some sharks also have **feelers** on their snouts that can sense tastes.

SHARK TAILS

Sharks use their tails for swimming—and even for catching prey!

Have I got a tale for you!

The tail of a great white shark is crescent-shaped.

Nurse shark

IS A SHARK **TAIL** LIKE **OTHER** FISH TAILS?

Both sharks and **bony fish** swish their tails when they swim. Both have two sections in their tails—an upper lobe and a lower lobe. A shark's **lobes** are often different sizes, while a bony fish's lobes are usually the same size. Another difference lies inside the tails. A shark's **backbone** extends into the upper lobe, but a bony fish's backbone doesn't.

Tiger shark

WHY DO DIFFERENT SHARK **SPECIES** HAVE DIFFERENT **TYPES** OF TAILS?

A shark's **tail** offers a clue to its lifestyle. A tiger shark's tail has a long, **pointed** upper lobe. The shape generates lots of power with every swish. The shark needs this power for swimming far and fast. A nurse shark has a long, **broad** tail that sweeps gently from side to side so it can cruise slowly along the seafloor.

Gray spiny dogfish

WHAT SHARK USES ITS TAIL TO **CATCH** ITS PREY?

The **thresher** shark has a whiplike tail that's as long as its body. It slaps its tail on the water to scare schools of fish so that they cluster together. Then the shark **whacks** at the fish with its tail. The smack stuns or injures the fish. Then it's a simple job for the shark to gobble up the confused fish. Sometimes these sharks also **wallop** seabirds floating on the water.

Thresher shark

21

THAT'S REALLY WILD!

There's something fishy about these sharks.

Newborn spined pygmy shark

THE **BIGGEST** SHARK

The **whale shark** is the world's biggest shark—and the world's biggest fish. The longest one ever measured was **45 feet**, but it's believed they can grow up to 60 feet. This **bus-size** shark is a gentle giant. It opens its 5-foot-wide mouth only to suck in water and filter out tiny food particles.

THE **SMALLEST** SHARK

The **dwarf lantern** shark is truly tiny! Males grow to just **6 inches** in length—about as long as a dollar bill. Females are a bit longer at 7.5 inches. This species lives in very deep parts of the Caribbean Sea. It wasn't discovered until 1985. Up until then, the award for smallest shark went to the spined **pygmy shark**, which is just a little bit longer.

Whale shark with scuba diver

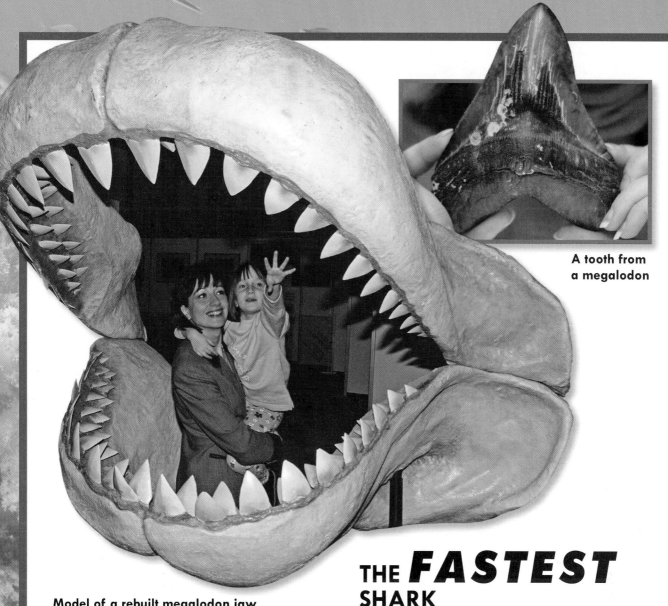

Model of a rebuilt megalodon jaw

A tooth from a megalodon

THE **BIGGEST** SHARK **EVER**

Until **2 million years ago**, an even bigger shark patrolled the oceans: **Megalodon**, a 60-foot-long beast that weighed about **77 tons**. That's about as much as 15 African elephants! Fossil teeth from this gigantic shark are nearly 7 inches long. Megalodon used those giant teeth to catch and eat fish—and whales, too.

THE **FASTEST** SHARK

The **shortfin mako**, a striking blue-backed, white-bellied shark, can swim at speeds up to **20 miles per hour**—about half as fast as a racehorse can run. This athletic shark can even **leap** out of the water. Being fast enables a mako to catch other swift swimmers, such as bluefish, tuna, and swordfish.

Mako shark

WHAT KIND OF SHARK IS THAT?

There are about 400 species of shark, with more waiting to be discovered.

I'm always ready to eat— I mean, *meet*— new sharks!

Sharks come in many sizes, shapes, and colors.

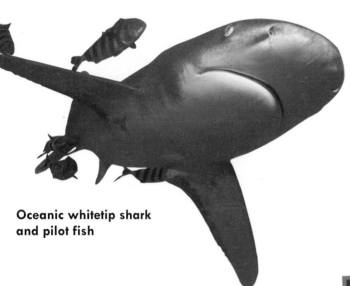

Oceanic whitetip shark and pilot fish

WHY ARE THERE **SO MANY SHARK SPECIES?**

Just like beetles, birds, mice, and other animals, different **kinds** of sharks are **adapted** to live in certain places and eat certain kinds of food. The ocean has many kinds of habitats and foods. Over many millions of years, sharks have adapted to them.

HOW DO SCIENTISTS **DISCOVER** NEW SHARK SPECIES?

New shark **species** may be found when scientists devote lots of time to exploring one specific place very thoroughly. That's how a new species of shark was discovered in the **Philippines** in **2011**. Never-before-seen sharks sometimes turn up in fishing nets, too. That's how scientists discovered a **rare** river shark in Borneo in 1997. In 2011, a new species of **dogfish** was discovered by a scientist visiting a fish market in Taiwan!

Oceanic whitetip shark swims past a scientist

Spiny dogfish

Stuffed megamouth shark

WHAT SHARK IS **VERY RARE?**

The **megamouth** shark is well known for not being well known! This rare species was discovered in **1976** when one got tangled in the anchor lines of a ship off the coast of **Hawaii**. Since then, fewer than 100 have been seen.

Great white shark

WHAT DO GREAT WHITES EAT?

A great white shark **eats** big—mainly seals, sea lions, dolphins, and fish. It even eats other sharks! The great white will swim close to its **prey**, then suddenly rush toward it and seize it with its **jaws**. If the prey is on the ocean's surface, the shark may shoot up through the water to grab it from below.

Great white shark

DOES A GREAT WHITE CHEW ITS FOOD?

The first thing you might notice about the great white is its big, **razor-sharp teeth**. It has 25 in its upper jaw, and another 25 in its lower jaw—and a whole bunch of backup teeth ready to take their place! They're not used for chewing, though. They're for grabbing and **sawing**, like knives. The shark clenches prey in its jaws, then shakes its head to **slice** up its meal.

WHY DO MOST SHARK ATTACKS INVOLVE GREAT WHITES?

They simply come into **contact** with people more than other sharks do. Great whites live and **hunt** mainly in the ocean's top layer, near shores of islands and continents. That's where people swim, surf, and dive. Great whites also check out anything that might be **edible**, often by taking a sample bite—which is bad news for the "anything" being sampled.

SHARKS
NO
SWIMMING

Mouth of a great white shark

THE GREAT WHITE'S STRANGE COUSINS

Great white sharks are in a group called mackerel sharks, along with makos and threshers. So are their "cousins," the unusual sharks you'll meet next!

Do I know these guys?

A basking shark looks like a great white shark, only bigger.

WHAT IS A BASKING SHARK?

The **basking shark** looks a bit like an extra-large great white. It's nearly 30 feet long! Only the whale shark is bigger. Its gill slits are so long, they seem to wrap around its head. The slits are lined with **gill rakers**. Unlike a megamouth, this shark doesn't suck up plankton-filled water. It just swims with its mouth wide open, **filtering** food from the sea as it goes.

Basking shark

WHAT IS A GOBLIN SHARK?

A **goblin shark** is a flabby, pinkish, snaggle-toothed shark with a long, flat, pointed **snout**. It can grow to be up to about 12 feet long. Its jaws are normally tucked into its head, but it **thrusts** them out to catch fish and squid. This shark lives deep in the ocean, so not much is known about it. Its long snout is packed with ampullae of Lorenzini. These electricity-sensing **pores** help the shark find prey on the dark seafloor.

Illustration of a goblin shark

WHAT IS A MEGAMOUTH?

A **megamouth** is a flabby, barrel-shaped brown shark with a bulb-shaped head and a mouth about **3 feet wide**. To eat, the shark opens its huge mouth and sucks in water filled with "plankton"— small, floating creatures, such as jellyfish, and tiny, shrimplike animals called krill. Brushy "**gill rakers**" trap the food before the water flows out of its gill slits. Only a few dozen of these **rare** sharks have been seen since the first one was discovered in 1976.

WIDE-EYED
AND *WEIRD*

There are about 9 species of hammerhead shark, each with its own oddly shaped head.

I never seem to find a hat that fits!

Hammerhead sharks are named for the unusual hammerlike shape of their heads.

Great hammerhead shark

Bonnethead

WHICH HAMMERHEADS ARE THE **BIGGEST** AND **SMALLEST?**

The **great hammerhead** measures up to **20 feet** long and can weigh up to 1,000 pounds. The smallest hammerhead is the 4-foot-long **bonnethead**. You guessed it—its head is shaped like a bonnet. (It's also known as a **shovelhead**, because it looks a bit like a shovel, too!)

HOW DO HAMMERHEADS SEE WITH **EYES** SO **FAR APART?**

Extremely well! A hammerhead's eyes not only sit far apart, they also **tilt** slightly forward. This way, what one eye sees overlaps a bit with what the other eye sees. This gives the shark "**binocular vision**" similar to ours, which makes it able to judge how far away things are. Other sharks' binocular vision isn't as good.

WHAT DO HAMMERHEADS **EAT?**

Great hammerheads eat **fish**, octopi, squid, and **stingrays**. They even eat the stingray's stinging tail! Big hammerheads also eat smaller hammerheads. Bonnetheads eat **crabs**, shrimp, **snails**, and little fish. Scientists are still learning more about the feeding habits of lesser-known species, such as the winghead shark.

Hammerhead shark

Great hammerhead shark

SPINNERS AND TIGERS AND BULLS, *OH, MY!*

The requiem-shark group includes a few species that are dangerous.

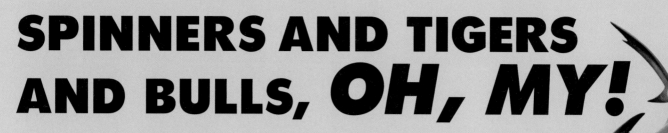

Sharks would really rather eat seafood, you know!

Tiger sharks eat all sorts of sea creatures, such as this conch shell and its soft inhabitant.

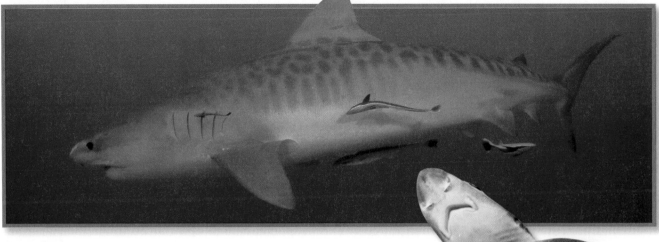

Tiger shark

WHAT DO TIGER SHARKS EAT?

Just about **everything**! These 20-foot-long sharks normally **prey** on sea turtles, fish, seabirds, dolphins, squids, and rays. They also eat dead sea animals. But scientists and fishermen have found all kinds of **junk** in tiger sharks' stomachs: cans, bottles, chunks of wood, bags of coal, sacks of potatoes, clothing, **car tires**, drums, boat cushions—even a chicken coop!

Spinner shark

WHICH SHARK *SPINS* LIKE A TOP?

The aptly named **spinner shark** spirals as it swims through schools of fish, snapping them up right and left. The shark moves so fast, it often **flies** out of the water and spins through the air.

WHICH SHARK SWIMS UP RIVERS?

Bull sharks live in shallow waters along coasts. They also swim into bays, harbors, and rivers. Bull sharks have even swum up the **Mississippi River** from Louisiana all the way north to Illinois— an 1,800-mile trip! Males reach 7 feet long. Females range up to 11 feet. Bull sharks swim in **coastal** waters in many places around the world. In the United States, they swim up the East Coast during summer. They can be found offshore near parts of California, too.

Bull shark

ANGEL SHARKS

About 15 species of angel shark lurk on the ocean floor.

Be careful where you step!

An angel shark's fins look like wings.

Pacific angel shark

WHAT IS AN ANGEL SHARK?

An **angel shark** looks like a flattened version of a typical shark. Its pectoral and pelvic fins look like wide, flat **wings**. Its mouth is at the tip of its head instead of underneath it, as with most sharks. Its eyes sit on top of its head rather than on the sides. Angel sharks grow to almost **5 feet** in length. They live along coastlines in many parts of the world.

HOW DO ANGEL SHARKS BREATHE?

An angel shark can breathe by using **muscles** in its mouth to suck in water and pump it across its **gills**. But this is hard to do if you're lying half-buried in sand and mud. Instead, the angel shark takes in water through a pair of slits on top of its head, called **spiracles**. The spiracles sit behind its eyes. Water taken in by the spiracles flows through tubes that lead to the gills.

WHY ARE ANGEL SHARKS FLAT?

Angel sharks spend a lot of time lying flat on the **seafloor**, partly hidden by sand, mud, and pebbles. Its speckled brown or gray body helps **camouflage** it, too. In this disguise, the shark waits for small fish, crabs, lobsters, and other animals to pass by. It catches the unsuspecting prey in its **sharp-toothed jaws**. If necessary, an angel shark may lie motionless for weeks to grab a meal!

Pacific angel shark

WOBBEGONGS DOWN UNDER

Wobbegongs belong to a group called carpet sharks, so named because many of them boast colorful patterns.

Do any of these carpets need cleaning?

Carpet sharks resemble colorful rugs.

WHAT IS A WOBBEGONG?

Wobbegongs have wide, flat bodies and heads. They live on the **seafloor** and in **coral reefs** in parts of the western Pacific Ocean and the eastern Indian Ocean. Australia, Japan, and Indonesia are some of the countries that have wobbegongs living along their coasts.

Illustration of ornate wobbegong

Tasseled wobbegong

Spotted wobbegong

WHY DO THEY HAVE SHAGGY FACES?

A wobbegong has fingerlike "**whiskers**" on its snout called **barbels**. These sense taste, touch, and electrical fields. Feathery fronds called **dermal lobes** hang from its mouth. The lobes ripple in the water, making the **camouflaged** shark look even more like part of the seafloor. Fish mistake the lobes for a seaweed dinner and quickly become the shark's dinner instead!

WHAT DO THEY **EAT?**

Crabs, lobsters, fish, shrimp, and octopi are among the **prey** eaten by wobbegongs. Like angel sharks, wobbegongs lie in the mud and sand of the seafloor, waiting to **ambush** prey. They may also **prowl** for meals. The spotted wobbegong may stalk its prey by crawling with its fins. A **tasseled** wobbegong attracts prey with its **beard**! It looks like food to bottom-dwelling fish. They come close to inspect it and become food in a flash!

WHALE SHARKS AND WALKING SHARKS

These wonderfully weird creatures are related to wobbegongs, so they're in the carpet-shark group, too.

And I thought sea stars were wild!

Whale sharks survive on a diet of mostly plankton.

DO WHALE SHARKS HAVE TEETH?

Whale sharks have about **3,000** tiny, sharp teeth in their massive mouths. The teeth are lined up in rows like seats in a movie theater. Whale sharks don't use their teeth for hunting or chewing, though. Instead, the sharks **filter** small prey—even microscopic critters—from the sea. They suck in water and strain it through **spongy** pads in their gill slits.

Whale shark

Whale shark feeding on plankton

WHAT ARE WALKING SHARKS?

Some kinds of small **carpet sharks** use their pectoral and pelvic fins as "legs." They are able to move their fins more freely than most sharks can. They resemble lizards as they **scamper** awkwardly across the seafloor. If startled, these sharks often run away instead of swimming to safety! The 3-foot-long **epaulette shark** is one species that goes for strolls.

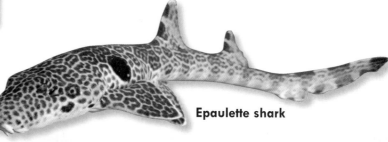
Epaulette shark

HOW DOES A WHALE SHARK LIVE ON A **DIET** OF **PLANKTON?**

It's amazing! The **whale shark** is the world's **biggest** fish, but it only eats tiny shrimp, fish eggs, very small fish, and ocean worms. Whale sharks spend nearly **8 hours** a day eating, gobbling up about **46 pounds** of plankton. A bigger whale shark probably eats even more!

Raja epaulette shark

THAT'S REALLY WILD!

We little guys gotta watch out for ourselves!

Big sharks don't worry much about predators, but small sharks do! Here are some amazing ways they defend themselves.

SPINES AND SPURS

Some small sharks who live on the seafloor have **spines** on their backs. Horn sharks and rough sharks both have a **venomous** spine in front of each dorsal fin. Spiny dogfish sharks have venomous spines, too. These spines are covered with a **germy slime** that infects the wounds they cause in attackers.

EYE SEE YOU!

The **epaulette shark** has a pair of big black spots on its back surrounded by white rings. The spots look very much like a big pair of **eyes**. These false eyes may make a predator think twice about attacking by making the shark look larger than the predator can handle.

Horn shark dorsal spine and fin

STICKY, PRICKLY

The **bramble shark**'s body is covered with **thorny** denticles and a **sticky**, stinky slime. Being a painful, nasty mouthful is a good way to avoid becoming a meal!

Camouflaged angel shark

CAMOUFLAGE

Some sharks **blend** in so well with their surroundings, they avoid becoming a meal for a bigger shark just by lying low. **Angel sharks** are colored like sand or mud, which helps them look like part of the seafloor. **Wobbegongs** have blotchy skin patterns that look like algae, seaweed, rocks, and coral.

HUFF AND PUFF

The **swell shark** is named for its defensive behavior. If a predator approaches, the swell shark curls up, grabs its tail in its mouth, and **gulps** water until it blows up to twice its normal size! The predator is so surprised, the swell shark has time to escape. The **tactic** works even better if the shark is hiding in a crevice when it swells up. It becomes wedged in so tightly, a predator can't yank it out.

Swell shark

Face of a swell shark

41

SAW SHARKS

There are about 9 species of saw-snouted shark slashing through the seas!

Saw sharks use their bladelike snouts and teeth to slash at prey.

Saw shark

WHAT IS A SAW SHARK'S
SAW FOR?

Like angel sharks and wobbegongs, **saw sharks** hunt on the seafloor. Their sawlike snouts are an adaptation for finding and feeding on prey. A saw shark skimming over a sandy seabed is like a swimming metal detector equipped with **whiskers** and a **chainsaw**!

Saw shark

Saw shark on the seafloor

HOW DOES THE SAW SHARK
KILL ITS PREY?

The **saw** may make up a third of the shark's length. It's lined with teeth on both sides! To kill hidden prey, the saw shark **jabs** its saw into the sand and whips its head back and forth. It also kills fish by **slashing** its saw in the water. Then the saw shark sucks the torn food into its mouth.

ARE THEY
DANGEROUS
TO PEOPLE?

The International Shark Attack File has records of shark attacks on people dating back to **1580**. None of these attacks was by a saw shark. These sharks are bottom-dwellers (animals that feed on the seabed), so people don't encounter them often. Also, saw sharks are pretty small—the biggest is no more than **5 feet long**. But any shark will bite if teased, grabbed, or stepped on. So it's best to leave a saw shark alone!

IT'S A *DOG!* IT'S A *FISH!* IT'S A...*DOGFISH!*

More than 100 species of sharks fall into the dogfish group.

Aw, please, Dad, can we get a dogfish?

These sharks are named for their pointy doglike snouts.

Dogfish

WHY ARE DOGFISH CALLED **DOGFISH?**

Dogfish may have earned this name because they have pointy **snouts**, like dogs. The name may also have been inspired by the way spiny dogfish sometimes **hunt** in packs, like wolves. Dozens of sharks may gather in a food-rich area and start **herding** prey, the way sheepdogs herd sheep. But sharks gobble up the creatures they herd!

Illustration of a lantern shark

HOW BIG ARE DOGFISH?

The **dwarf lantern shark**, at 6 to 7.5 inches long, is both the **smallest** dogfish and the smallest shark species. The **biggest** dogfish is the **Greenland shark**, which measures 21 feet from snout to tail—about the size of a great white. Greenland sharks live in the North Atlantic Ocean, where they eat fish and whales.

WHAT MAKES **GREENLAND SHARKS** UNUSUAL?

Many shark species live **deep** in cold oceans, but just a few swim in the icy waters at Earth's poles. One of them is the Greenland shark, the only shark known to cruise under the ice sheets covering **Arctic waters**. It can stand such cold water because it has a **chemical** in its blood that keeps its body fluids from freezing. It has so much of this chemical that Greenland shark meat is poisonous to humans!

Diver with a Greenland shark

Greenland shark

THE COOKIECUTTER SHARK

This little shark is one tough cookie!

One dogfish, the cookiecutter, is probably the strangest shark of all!

Cookiecutter sharks use their mouths to cut into their prey.

WHY IS IT CALLED A "COOKIECUTTER" SHARK?

Cookiecutter sharks are named for their bizarre feeding habits. This little shark, just **1½ feet long**, preys on squid, large fish, sharks, seals, dolphins, and even whales! It's too small to kill them, of course. Instead, it **scoops** chunks of flesh the size of ping-pong balls from their bodies!

Illustration of cookiecutter sharks feeding on dolphin

WHAT OTHER **TRICKS** DOES A COOKIECUTTER **HAVE?**

It may be able to **attract** prey. A cookiecutter's belly is packed with light-producing organs, except for a patch beneath its gill slits. The **glowing** belly blends in with light trickling down from the water's surface, which makes the dark spot more noticeable. As a result, the spot resembles a very small fish, perhaps **luring** a predator to come closer and check it out. Then the cookiecutter quickly chomps a chunk from its side.

HOW DOES A COOKIECUTTER CUT?

First the cookiecutter shark "**kisses**" the body of its prey with its big, rubbery lips. Then it raises a tonguelike bump of **cartilage** in its throat so that its mouth works like a suction cup. Once the shark is clamped on, it jams its sawlike lower teeth into its prey, then stabs with its **spiky** upper teeth. Finally, with a twist of its body, the shark gouges out a blob of flesh.

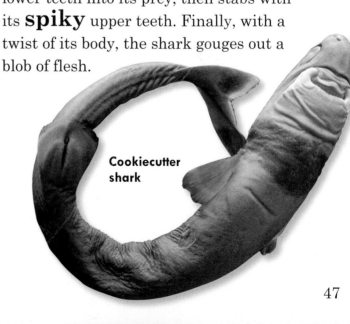

Cookiecutter shark

THAT'S REALLY WILD!

☐ **TRUE**

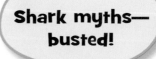

Shark myths—busted!

OR

☐ **FALSE**

ALL SHARKS MUST SWIM NONSTOP OR THEY'LL SINK LIKE A ROCK.

FALSE! Adaptations such as big pectoral **fins**, oily livers, and **lightweight** cartilage skeletons help sharks float. So even though sharks tend to sink if they don't swim, they sink very **slowly**. Some sharks *want* to sink. Sharks that feed on the seafloor don't want to bob up to the surface!

Leopard shark

ALL SHARKS MUST SWIM NONSTOP TO BREATHE.

FALSE! Most shark species are able to use their mouth and throat **muscles** to pump water in and out. Angel sharks and other seafloor dwellers use their **spiracles** to take in water while lying flat on sand and mud. Some fast-swimming, open-ocean sharks, such as **hammerheads** and great whites, *do* swim constantly, though. They must do this to breathe by forcing water into their mouths and over their gills.

Shark fin

Lemon shark

SHARK CARTILAGE IS AN AMAZING CURE-ALL.

FALSE! People once believed that sharks never got cancer, and that this trait was linked to having a cartilage **skeleton**. That's why some people buy shark-cartilage pills. But sharks actually do develop tumors. It's true that sharks **recover** very quickly from wounds, but so far scientists haven't found that this ability is linked to a "**wonder chemical**."

SHARKS EAT ANYTHING AND EVERYTHING.

FALSE! Most sharks are fussy about food. Their teeth, bodies, and hunting behaviors are **adapted** for finding and eating certain kinds of prey. Great whites are adapted for killing and eating seals and sea lions. Most of the time, if a great white **bites** a human, it doesn't come back for a second bite. A fat seal is a better meal than a bony person. Even tiger sharks, known for swallowing **garbage** they find in the sea, are really just looking for prey such as fish.

Blacktip shark

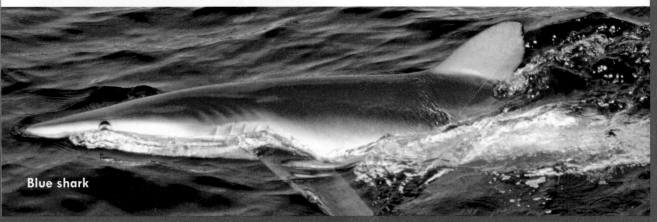

Blue shark

SHARK REPRODUCTION

Sharks give birth to their babies—called pups—in three different ways!

Some sharks lay eggs while others give birth to live pups.

I remember when you were just a cute little egg.

DO SHARKS LAY EGGS?

Cat sharks, carpet sharks, and horn sharks are among the shark species that lay eggs. These eggs have a **leathery** outside instead of a hard shell like birds' eggs. The tough outside hardens after the egg is laid and is bathed in seawater. A single **shark pup** develops inside each egg. Depending on the species, it takes 6 to 12 months for the pup to grow and hatch.

Dogfish egg

Cat shark egg

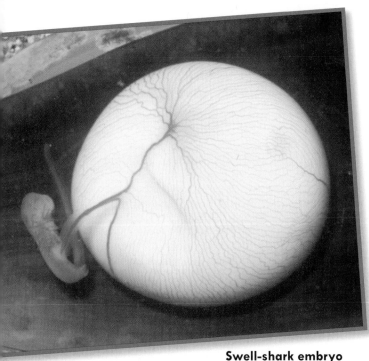

Swell-shark embryo

WHAT DO SHARK EGGS LOOK LIKE?

Many sharks lay **boxy** eggs with strings at each end. The **strings** get tangled in seaweed. As they harden in the seawater, they shrink, which ties the eggs to the seaweed tightly until the pup hatches. Some sharks, such as the Port Jackson shark and the horn shark, lay spiral-shaped eggs! These eggs twist into sand or among rocks like **screws**.

DO SHARKS GIVE BIRTH TO PUPS?

Most sharks are "**live-bearers**," which means they give birth to live pups instead of laying **eggs**. Sharks have two ways of doing this. Some species produce soft, thin-shelled eggs that stay inside their bodies. The pups develop in these eggs, **hatch** inside their moms, and then are born. Other live-bearers have pups that grow inside their bodies, but not inside eggs. A live-bearer may **carry** her pups for 9 to 24 months, depending on the species.

Shark egg case

SHARK PUPS

Shark pups know how to swim, eat, and fend for themselves right from the start.

Aww, how cute! A baby bonnethead!

This bonnethead pup can already take care of itself.

Swell shark emerging from egg case

Four-day-old whitetip shark

DO SHARK PUPS HAVE TEETH?

Shark pups are hatched or born with **teeth** and are ready to eat and take care of themselves right away. In some species, pups use their teeth even before they're born! A **thresher** shark, for example, makes extra eggs in her body for her unborn pups to eat. The **sand tiger** has an even more unusual system. She may have 40 pups growing inside her, but she only gives birth to one or two pups. That's because the biggest ones eat their smaller **siblings** before they're born!

HOW MANY PUPS DOES A SHARK HAVE?

Bony fish lay thousands, even **millions** of eggs all at once. Egg-laying sharks don't. **Horn sharks** and small-spotted cat sharks, for example, lay just 20 to 24 eggs per year. Live-bearers have anywhere from two pups (such as the sand tiger) to **300** (such as the whale shark). Sharks do not take care of their pups after hatching or birth.

HOW **BIG** ARE **PUPS?**

Pups **range in size** from just a few inches long (such as lantern-shark pups) to basking-shark pups that are nearly 6 feet long! **Lantern sharks** range in size from 6 to 10 inches or so as adults, while a **basking shark** pup may grow to nearly 30 feet.

Dogfish pups

SHARK HANGERS-ON

Most sea creatures avoid sharks—but there are some that hang out with them all the time!

C'mon—let's go for a swim!

The remora fish is sometimes called a sucker fish.

WHAT FISH **ATTACH** THEMSELVES TO SHARKS?

A fish called the **sharksucker**, or **remora**, has a disk on its head that works like a **suction cup**. It uses the disk to stick itself to a shark's skin. It can let go whenever it wants, but it mostly rides along with the shark. The little fish eat scraps from the shark's meals. They also pay the shark back by eating smaller pests that live on the shark's skin, such as little shrimplike creatures called **copepods**.

Sucker fish holding on by suction cup–like organs

Remoras on a shark

DO **COPEPODS** HARM SHARKS?

Copepods certainly don't *help* sharks! They **burrow** into a shark's skin, leaving their rear ends sticking out. Then they eat fluids, such as mucus, produced by the shark's skin. Some copepods **nibble** the shark's skin itself or even feed on its blood. The **Greenland** shark's vision is harmed by copepods that **cling** to its eyes. If you see a shark with what looks like streamers flying from its fins, it is carrying a load of copepods trailing their bannerlike egg cases.

DO SHARKS NEED FISH TO **GUIDE THEM** TO FOOD?

People used to think sharks were so stupid, they needed schools of striped **pilot fish** to lead them to prey. Today, scientists think pilot fish swim with sharks for a few reasons. First, pilot fish are just programmed to swim in **schools**—even if their "schoolmate" is a shark! Pilot fish also eat **scraps** from the shark's meals. They may also save energy by riding on the ripples of water produced by the shark's swimming action.

◀ Whitetip shark with pilot fish

SHARK RELATIVES

Sharks have boatloads of cousins in the ocean! They are related to skates, rays, and fish called chimeras.

Hey! Is that my teacher, Mr. Ray?

Rays, such as this spotted eagle ray, have fins that look like wings.

Manta ray

HOW MANY KINDS OF SKATES AND RAYS ARE THERE?

Between **500 and 600**. Some of the best known species are the manta ray, which measures up to 27 feet across; stingrays, which have **venomous** spines on their tails; electric rays, which have **electric** organs that zap both prey and predators; and sawfish, which are sharklike rays with long, **toothy** snouts much like a saw shark's saw.

WHAT ARE SKATES AND RAYS?

Skates and rays are **flat-bodied** fish that look a bit like angel sharks. Their pectoral fins resemble **wings**. These are attached along the head and body. Skates and rays swim mainly by moving these "wings." Like sharks, skates and rays have skeletons made of **cartilage**. Unlike sharks, their gill slits are on their undersides.

Blue spotted stingray

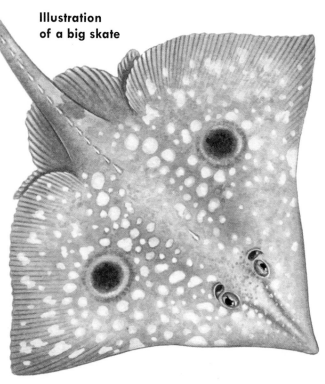
Illustration of a big skate

HOW DO SKATES AND RAYS DIFFER?

The biggest difference is that skates lay **eggs**, while rays give birth to live young. Many skates also have a clearly visible **dorsal** fin, but rays either have small ones or none at all. Skates have thick, **spineless tails**, while most rays have whiplike tails equipped with spines. Skates are usually smaller than rays.

SHARKS AND PEOPLE

Many people fear sharks. Many others admire them.

I have a lot of self-respect.

Sharks are often found on view in aquariums.

ARE SHARKS DANGEROUS?

All sharks **bite**, so it's smart to think of any shark as potentially **dangerous**. Swimmers, divers, and boaters are wise to learn about sharks and avoid attacks. But actual shark **attacks** on humans are **rare**. Every year, about 70 to 100 shark attacks are reported worldwide, with perhaps 5 to 15 causing death. Far more people fall victim to other dangers. **Car crashes** alone take the lives of about 37,000 people a year in the United States.

WHERE CAN PEOPLE SEE LIVE SHARKS?

Some species, such as lemon sharks, survive well in **captivity**. These sharks are often on view in **aquariums**. People can also see live sharks in the wild. Tour boats in places such as Hawaii and South Africa take people out to sea to places where sharks are plentiful. Some people even enter the water inside **shark-proof cages** to see sharks up close.

Divers photographing a shark through a shark cage

DO PEOPLE EAT SHARKS?

Yes! One of the most widely consumed shark species is the spiny dogfish. People also use other parts of the shark to make products. Shark skin, for example, is turned into **leather**. Liver oil has been used to make **cosmetics** and to make oils that keep machines running smoothly. Scientists also study shark chemicals for use as **medicines**.

◀ **Zebra shark in a tank**

THE FUTURE
OF SHARKS

About one third of
shark species are in
danger of extinction.

Our fate is in
human hands?
I didn't see
that coming!

Millions of
sharks are
caught every
year.

WHY ARE SHARKS IN DANGER?

Every year, between 26 million and 73 million sharks are **caught** at sea, either accidentally (in nets set out to catch other fish) or on purpose. Sadly, most sharks caught on purpose are **killed** just for their fins in a process called **finning**. The fins are used to make shark-fin soup, which is an Asian specialty.

WHAT WOULD OCEANS BE LIKE WITHOUT SHARKS?

Sharks are "**apex predators**." That means they're at the top of the food heap, like lions or eagles. They keep populations of prey animals in check. A study in 2007 found that when too many big sharks along the East Coast of the U.S. were caught, **populations** of cow-nose rays (a favorite shark food) increased. The rays, in turn, gobbled up bay scallops, an important food for other **wildlife** as well as people. Sharks are a **vital** part of the ocean's well-being. Their predatory ways help keep a balance among sea creatures.

WHAT'S BEING DONE TO PROTECT SHARKS?

In some countries, **laws** have been passed that ban finning, selling fins, or serving shark-fin soup. Finning is illegal in the United States. It's also illegal to ship shark fins into the country. Some countries have even set up **sanctuaries** for sharks and other sea creatures. The nation of Honduras, in Central America, for example, **banned** shark fishing in its waters in 2011.

GLOSSARY

Ampullae of Lorenzini: sensory organs in a shark's head that detect low levels of electricity given off by other animals

Barbels: sensory organs on a shark's face used for tasting and touching

Bony fish: fish that have skeletons made of bone

Cartilage: a flexible material that forms a shark's skeleton

Caudal fin: a shark's tail

Dermal denticles: toothlike structures in a shark's skin

Dorsal fin: an upright fin on a shark's back

Extinct: no longer in existence; an extinct species is one that has disappeared forever

Finning: catching and killing sharks just for their fins for use in specialty foods

Gill rakers: structures in the gills of filter-feeding sharks that strain food from water

Gill slits: a series of five, six, or seven slits on the sides of a shark's head that house its gills

Gills: breathing structures on sharks and other fish that take in oxygen from the water and release carbon dioxide into it

Habitat: the environment in which a shark lives

Lateral lines: strips of sensory cells on a fish's sides that are sensitive to motion

Overfishing: removing more sharks from the ocean than the species can produce

Plankton: small, floating animals and plantlike organisms in the ocean

Predator: an animal that eats other animals

Prey: an animal that is eaten by another animal

Ram-jet ventilation: a method of breathing used by some sharks that involves swimming constantly in order to force water into the mouth and through the gills

Spiracles: nostril-like openings on a shark's head that are used for breathing

Streamlined: shaped to slip quickly and easily through water

Swim bladder: a balloonlike organ inside a fish that helps it float

Venomous: able to inject venom, a toxic substance made by an animal's body

INDEX

PHOTO CREDITS